Anoushka's
Extraordinary Heroes

Anoushka's Extraordinary Heroes

Library of Cingress Cataloging-in-Publication Data is available upon request.

Book Cover by Oliver Bundoc
Illustrations by Oliver Bundoc

First edition, 2023

For the bright star that is Anoushka who shines her light and love in all the dark places.

Thank you.

"Hello, my name is Anoushka. My heroes are the most extraordinary people in the world. Let me introduce them to you. I hope you think they are as cool as I do. Flip the page and follow me."

> ### *"Every life matters regardless of the number of chromosomes we have."*

Karen was born in Mountain View, California, before her parents moved the family to Portland, Oregon. When she was a baby, her mommy would sit her in the tub and blow air in her face so Karen would hold her breath before her mommy poured water over her head. She was already learning an important part of swimming before she was one year old!

Soon, she was going to the pool on the weekends with her daddy. She would play a game where she would sit on the bottom of the pool and measure the breath she had left to get safely out of the water. With her daddy's help, she grew to love the water, whether in the tub, the pool, or the ocean.

Growing up, Karen had two dreams: to be a champion swimmer and to earn her high school diploma. Karen received her high school diploma, earned a two-year college degree, and is the first person with Down syndrome to have an honorary doctorate degree! She is Dr. Karen Gaffney. Although she does not fix people, she works hard to fix how they see people with Down syndrome. She travels to many cities around the world to tell everyone that people like her are more alike rather than different from everyone else. Her other claim to fame is that she is the first person with Down syndrome to deliver a TED Talk.

Karen is an amazing swimmer who is very unlike other swimmers since she uses mostly her upper body instead of her legs to push through the water. She is the first person with Down syndrome to swim the English Channel as part of a six-person relay team. The winner of two gold medals from the Special Olympics, she has completed sixteen swims across the San Francisco Bay, a nine-mile solo swim across the width of Lake Tahoe, an eight-and-a-half-mile swim across Lake Champlain, and a five-mile swim from Molokai to Wailea Beach in Maui, Hawaii, just to name a few. All the swimming events to which Karen lends her talents are always for the purpose of raising awareness about the amazing abilities of people living with Down syndrome.

Karen is some of the best things to be in the world – committed, intentional, and outspoken.

Karen Gaffney

"Each impossible mission can be made possible if you put your mind to it and work hard without giving up."

When Sujeet was a little boy in Syracuse, New York, he did not understand why he could not keep up with all the other little boys and girls. His mommy and daddy explained to him that he was capable of learning like the other kids, but he just needed a little more time. He remembered what his parents told him and did his very best. He graduated from high school with honors, and attended college at the Berkshire Hills Music Academy.

Sujeet is an expert musician. When he was nine years old, his parents signed him up for violin lessons to help with his memory and his hand-eye coordination. Often, he would go with his mommy to wait for his brother to finish his piano lessons, and then he would come home and play the tunes he heard. He had an amazing memory.

Soon, he was also playing piano, then taking clarinet lessons, and before long, he had taught himself how to play several other instruments like the bass clarinet and saxophone, as well as the drums. In total, he has mastered seven instruments—Bb and bass clarinets, alto saxophone, violin, piano, trumpet, and drums. He is the first person with Down syndrome to play at the Carnegie Hall, a concert venue where only the very best are allowed to play their instruments. Sujeet has performed in nearly all the states in America and thirteen different countries!

A great sportsman, Sujeet has a black belt in Tae Kwon Do, a sport he started at eight years old and continues to practice today. He has won gold and silver medals in the Special Olympics World Games in alpine skiing, swimming, cross-country running, and bowling. A recipient of numerous awards for his advocacy, two documentary films have been made about Sujeet's life, along with many TV and newspaper interviews. He has appeared as a guest on national television shows like The View and The Oprah Winfrey Show.

Sujeet has worked as a teacher's aide, and a music and basic computer skills instructor. Living independently with his wife, he continues to inspire everyone around him through his music in community churches, nursing homes, senior centers, and hospitals, bringing joy to those away from home and family.

Sujeet is some of the best things to be in the world – optimistic, helpful, and well-spoken.

Madeline Stuart

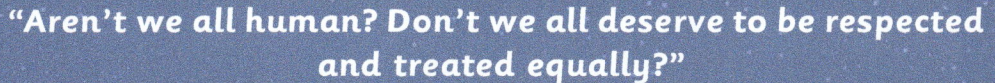

"Aren't we all human? Don't we all deserve to be respected and treated equally?"

"Mum, me model," said Madeline to her mom as she watched the beautiful models in amazement at her first fashion runway show. Madeline was born in Brisbane, Australia. Her mom told her every day that she was beautiful and capable, so Madeline always believed that she could achieve anything she set her mind on.

She knew that if she wanted to become a fashion model, she would have to work hard, eat her fruits and vegetables, exercise, and practice her catwalk. She did such a great job that her mom rewarded her with a professional hair and makeup session, and a photoshoot! Madeline's pictures were so beautiful that many newspapers around the world wanted to know about her. She was invited to be a model at the famous New York Fashion Week, making her one of the first professional adult models with Down syndrome.

Since then, Madeline Stuart has walked on runways in cities like Paris, London, and Dubai. Many important magazines and newspapers like Vogue, Cosmopolitan, Elle, Marie Claire, Forbes, and the New York Times have written about her. She has won many awards for her modeling and her work in making sure the world is kind and fair to people with disabilities.

Madeline is some of the best things to be in the world – confident, focused, and determined.

"It's not about celebrating disabilities; it's about celebrating abilities."

When Chris was born in Point Lookout, New York, so little was known about Down syndrome that his mommy and daddy were told not to take him home. But they did! They chose to nurture him with the same love and attention they gave to his siblings, who really liked having a baby brother. While his siblings went to school, Chris had to go to a special school for differently-abled people, because at that time regular schools did not make space for people with different learning abilities. After graduation, he worked as an elevator operator and did volunteer work for programs for students with disabilities.

Chris always knew what he wanted to do when he grew up: he wanted to be on TV one day! His parents encouraged him to follow his dream even though they had never seen anyone with Down syndrome on television or in the movies. His first performance was in a play called The Emperor's New Clothes at his special school. He did such an amazing job that he impressed not only the audience but also an important Hollywood movie producer. This great reception made Chris want to do better, so he continued to learn and practice by attending night classes, going to auditions, writing scripts, and hungrily reading books about his favorite actors.

His hard work was rewarded with his first professional acting job in a movie on a major TV network. His bosses were so happy with his performance that they created a show called Life Goes On, and made his character, Charles "Corky" Thatcher, the main character! This made Chris the first person (and Corky the first character) in a network television series with Down syndrome. His realistic portrayal of people with Down syndrome changed the way people around the world looked at people with disabilities.

When he is not touring with his three-piece musical group, "Chris Burke with Joe and John DeMasi," he makes public appearances, speaks with the press, greets fans, and gives inspirational speeches as a Goodwill Ambassador for the National Down Syndrome Society (NDSS). He is also a valued staff member at the NDSS New York Office.

Chris is some of the best things to be in the world – hard-working, likable, and intuitive.

Chris Burke

LIFE
GOES ON

"I don't really like that word 'retard,' because it puts people down, people with disabilities, and whenever I talk about it, it makes me a little bit emotional. Let the public know that using the R-word is not acceptable."

These strong words were spoken by Melissa in support of the government bill that will remove all references of the R-word to describe people with intellectual or developmental disabilities in documents. Born in Acton, Massachusetts, she graduated from high school and received a certificate in Business and Office support from the Transition Program at Middlesex Community College.

Melissa has always been surrounded by love and support being the youngest of four children. She never felt left out; her siblings' friends were also her friends, and she was included in travel and outing plans. Because she was privileged to always be in an inclusive environment, she has made advocating for employment and a more inclusive world for people like herself a priority.

Melissa understands that the only way to make real change is through getting involved in local politics, so she boldly called Senator Jamie Eldridge and asked if she could work as his intern. Since 2013, she has been a valued team member that handles database entry, record maintenance for constituent services, and other administrative tasks as an aide in the senator's office at the Massachusetts State House. In addition to her Beacon Hill job, Melissa works as a classroom assistant at the Learning Program Boston, a preschool for children with Down syndrome.

When she is not working and teaching, Melissa devotes her time to the Special Olympics where she started to compete at just eight years old. She showed a talent for competition, participating in swimming, cycling, and skiing. She has participated in two Special Olympics World Winter Games, competing in alpine skiing. To acknowledge Melissa's athletic and leadership accomplishments, Special Olympics Massachusetts inducted her into the Special Olympics Massachusetts Hall of Fame in 2010.

A recipient of several awards, and featured in magazines, newspapers, and TV and radio programs, Melissa is a global messenger and a sought-after keynote speaker who uses her position to encourage people to think about individuals with Down syndrome and other disabilities as able and capable. Like she has said in one of many presentations, she is a regular girl who happens to have Down syndrome.

Melissa is some of the best things to be in the world – a leader, adventurous, and exemplary.

Melissa Reilly

Emmett Kyoshi Wilson

"*I like to paint because I dream. I feel, like, a passion. I feel proud.*"

Born and raised in Glenview, Illinois, Emmett's mommy and daddy did not know that he rocked the extra chromosome until five days after he was born. When he was four, he did not have an easy time drawing, writing, or speaking like other kids. One day, his mommy gave him a giant poster board, paints, and brushes, and like magic, everything Emmett could not draw, write, or speak flowed freely in a burst of strokes, swirls, and colors. His parents were so proud of him, especially his daddy, who is also a painter. They started showing Emmett's work at galleries and selling them online.

Since the age of four, Emmett has created over eighty abstract pieces that have been presented in three official gallery shows. He has been commissioned to produce special works, like painting the American flag for the United States Embassy in Croatia and creating a new logo for the company Optimizely.

To Emmett, it is not only important to spread the message of inclusion, and raise awareness and understanding about Down syndrome, it is necessary to give back to the community. Emmett's parents have established Hair Cares NFP, a nonprofit that gives back to underserved members of their community through sales of his paintings, fashion shows, coat drives, raffles, and more.

Since 2017, he has raised over $75,000 for various charities such as the National Association for Down syndrome (NAD), The Jackson Chance Foundation, Rags of Honor, and The Greater Chicago Food Depository. A recipient of the Soaring Spirit Award from Looking Beyond LA, he has been featured as a young creator in Disney's Diversity and an inclusion initiative called 'Reimagine Tomorrow' as well as Adobe Max's 2021 Virtual Conference. Emmett's work has been featured on 'In the Know', NBC Chicago, and more.

Emmett is some of the best things to be in the world – expressive, spontaneous, and generous.

"My right to be born."

The right to live is the reason that Emmanuel says self-advocacy is important to him. It is why he presents his life story as an example of what kids with Down syndrome can achieve when they are given the chance.

Born in Grafton, Illinois, Emmanuel showed everyone how smart he was by sight reading flashcards in French at age three, which made his mommy and daddy very proud. At age six, Emmanuel started playing the violin which was a wonderful surprise to his parents since they did not know how to play any instruments. By twelve years old, he was chosen to perform at the 10th World Down Syndrome Congress in Ireland. Since then, he has played with many symphony orchestras, string quartets, and quintets at eleven basilicas and cathedrals.

Emmanuel is fluent in English, French, Spanish and Latin. When he was six years old, he gave a welcome speech to six-hundred people in three languages at the National Down Syndrome Society annual meeting. He is an impressive speaker that has traveled to twenty-five countries to tell everyone that people with Down syndrome are capable of amazing things when low expectations are replaced by high hopes.

When he is not speaking to crowds of people or making magical music with his violin, he loves swimming and playing golf. He has won twenty-eight gold, nine silver, and four bronze medals in both sports.

Emmanuel is some of the best things to be in the world – disciplined, ambitious, and smart.

Emmanuel Bishop

Megan Bomgaars

"Don't Limit Me!"

Megan declared these three important words in a video she created in high school, and it got her an invitation to the White House to attend the Beating the Odds Summit with First Lady Michelle Obama.

Born in Denver, Colorado, Megan was first noticed while giving an important speech at a National Down Syndrome Congress meeting. She did such a great job that she was asked to be an actress on a show about people with Down syndrome called Born This Way. Along with her castmates, she showed the world that people with Down syndrome have a purpose, a wish to do work they love, and that they can meet realistic (but not impossible) expectations.

Since she has been on the show, Megan has worked with the Hello Kitty brand to create custom tee shirts, lipsticks for Artpop Cosmetic under a collection called "Don't Limit Me," and was included in the We Belong to Something Beautiful campaign by Sephora cosmetics. With those three words, "Don't Limit Me," she let the world know that people with disabilities bloom best in inclusive environments, and that they also want a seat at the table.

Megan is some of the best things to be in the world – inspirational, passionate, and observant.

"Don't give up... don't ever give up. It's easy to make excuses and quit. I don't do excuses, and I don't quit...
because my dream is bigger than my pain."

When Chris was born in Maitland, Florida, his mommy, and daddy were told not to expect him to amount to much of anything. It was not a very nice thing to say to new parents. But this seemed true for some time when he had open surgery at five months old, was not able to walk well until four years old, or eat solid food until age five. By age seventeen, he had four major ear operations and still struggled with balance, slow reaction time, and low muscle tone. At eighteen, Chris did not know what he wanted to do until the Special Olympics started a triathlon program in Florida. This led to his a-ha moment. His parents encouraged him to join, get in shape, but above all have fun.

Soon enough, Chris outgrew his first triathlon coach, and with his next coach, he went from TV surfing on the couch to sprinting a fourteen-mile triathlon! Until he came along, no person with Down syndrome had ever attempted to participate in the Ironman Race, which is seventeen hours and consists of cycling (for 112 miles/180.25km), swimming (for 2.4 miles/3.86km) and running (for 26.22 miles/42.20km). Talk about a lot of exercise!

At twenty-one years old, he completed the Ironman Florida triathlon in sixteen hours, forty-six minutes, and nine seconds. This accomplishment earned him recognition from Guinness World Records, the Jimmy V Award for Perseverance, Best Athlete with a Disability in Men's Sport (both part of the ESPY Award), and the Laureus Sporting Moment of the Year Award.

He has made over forty appearances as a public speaker, and received an Adidas sponsorship and a new book deal. His new book explains the strategy behind his success—getting better 1% at a time each day..

Chris is some of the best things to be in the world – steadfast, philosophical, and consistent.

Chris Nikic

"She was just Judy to me; I didn't think of her as different at all. As we got older, I started realizing that people in the neighborhood treated her differently. That was my first thought, that people treated her badly." ~Joyce Wallace Scott

Judith was born with her fraternal twin in Cincinnati, Ohio, but unlike her sister, she was rocking the extra chromosome and was diagnosed with Down syndrome. When she was a baby, she suffered from scarlet fever which impaired her hearing. This was a secret only Judith knew but was unable to share with her mommy and daddy or sister.

Because she was unable to hear and so unable to speak, when her mommy and daddy tried to put her in school with her sister, they were told that she was not someone that could be educated. They were told they had to put her in a special place for people like her. Her sister was sad when she woke up in the morning and Judy was gone. She worried that Judy would be forgotten. Thirty-five years after that sudden separation, her sister found out that Judy could not hear all along. She was made her legal guardian and the wonder twins were back together again.

Two years after returning to the loving arms of her family, Judith began to attend the Creative Growth Art Center, one of the first organizations in the world to provide studio space for artists with disabilities to express themselves. At first, she did not like any of the activities until she saw a class in fiber art and something in her opened up. She developed a connection to the yarns and other random objects that she turned into her own spontaneous, unique, and colorful expression of art. Judith never ever repeated a form or color scheme. Today, her work is now counted amongst notable contemporary artists selling for substantial sums of money. Judith, who was always an outsider, had finally found a place to fit in. Her art is held in the permanent collections of many great museums such as the Museum of Modern Art, Museum of American Folk Art, etc.

After ten years of working on her art form, Judith was given her first exhibition which, coupled with a book about her work, caught the attention and acclaim of the international art community. She soon became the subject of four documentaries in three languages.

Judith is some of the best things to be in the world – imaginative, cherished, and respected.

Judith Scott

Tim Harris

"I have Down syndrome and I'm awesome."

There has never been anyone who has met Tim and not come away with a spirit-lifting hug. He grew up in Albuquerque, New Mexico, where he was named Homecoming King and Student of the Year. After high school, he graduated from university with certificates in Food Service, Office Skills, and Restaurant Hosting. He loved working as a restaurant host at his first job, and while he loved meeting many new people, Tim had a big dream to own a restaurant, too. He even knew that hugs would be on the menu, right after dessert! In 2010, his parents gave that dream wings and "Tim's Place" was opened, making him the first person with Down syndrome to own and operate a restaurant.

Tim worked at the restaurant six days a week. It became a place where people went for great food and left with a full heart. One of the happy recipients of Tim's famous hugs was President Barack Obama! Tim was also invited to introduce First Lady Michelle Obama at the opening ceremonies of the Special Olympics World Games before 60,000 people and a world-wide television audience. This amazing opportunity made Tim realize how important it was to carry his message of positivity, love, and inspiration to everyone to encourage them to identify and follow their dreams. A motivational and inspirational speaker, he has been featured in many magazines and networks. He is the recipient of the Quincy Jones Exceptional Advocacy Award.

Tim is some of the best things to be in the world – cheerful, positive, and fearless.

Isabella Springmuhl Tejada

"It was a No that I wanted to turn into a big YES."

Born in Guatemala City, Guatemala, Isabella would watch her abuela make beautiful clothes. She loved her abuela so much and she wanted to be just like her. At age six, Isabella started drawing and making clothes for her dolls. After high school, she knew exactly what she wanted to be: a Fashion Designer!

When she graduated from college, Isabella applied to study fashion design at a college in her town, but she was told "No." She did not let that stop her! She had a dream to make beautiful clothes like her abuela. There was also something extra special about her dream; she wanted to make beautiful clothes for people like herself, people with Down syndrome.

With a talent so big and bright, and the support of her family, Isabella worked hard to make her design collection Down to Xjabelle a reality. Inspired by her identity, upbringing, and culture, Isabella's colorful clothes earned her a spot as the first fashion designer with Down syndrome to display her designs at the International Design Showcase at London Fashion Week. And she was only nineteen years old!

Isabella is some of the best things to be in the world – thoughtful, creative, and persistent.

Eli Reimer

"It was surreal to be standing there at that place and see the smile on Eli's face and the sense of accomplishment that he had, and the fact that his health was better than any of us at that point ... it was humbling, it was inspiring, just an amazing moment." ~Justin Reimer

Eli is from Bend, Oregon, and when he was born with Down syndrome, his four siblings could not wait to welcome him home. They wanted to teach him all the fun things about being a kid in the big, big, world, like snowshoeing, cross-country skiing, basketball, and football. When his mommy and daddy found out that Eli would be born with Down syndrome, they decided to start a foundation called The Elisha Foundation to show the love and support they give to Eli, to other members of their community, and people throughout the world with special needs.

One day, a friend of Eli's mommy and daddy who likes to trek long distances said he wanted to climb to the Mount Everest base camp to raise money for a good cause. Eli also decided that he wanted to do the same thing and help raise money for the foundation. He never thought for once that he could not meet the challenge and his family believed in him. Everyone that heard about Eli and his journey were very excited for him.

Eli and his daddy trained in the Cascades for a year to get ready for the seventy-mile hike in the Himalayan mountains. During the journey, when everyone on the trek was feeling tired, Eli led them on the trail like a superhero. He gave everyone else the inspiration to keep going up, up, up.

Then one day, there it was...the South Base Camp of the mountain, which sits at 17,600 feet! The trek took ten days to complete. Eli, his daddy, and six other climbers raised $85,000 for the Elisha Foundation. This money helped them be able to continue the great work of providing services to families who love someone with a disability. At fifteen years old, he is the first person with Down syndrome to reach Mt. Everest's Base Camp.

Eli is some of the best things to be in the world – faithful, healthy, and persevering.

"Zumba is for everybody; everyone can do it."

Yulissa is a Peruvian-born resident of San Francisco, California, who fell in love with dancing as a one-year-old at a party. Even when the music stopped, Yulissa kept dancing! It was no surprise that after attending a Zumba class, she was hooked. She boldly told everyone that she was going to be a certified Zumba instructor one day. There had never been a Zumba instructor with Down syndrome, but that did not stop Yulissa. Every day she would memorize and practice her routines for six hours.

Four years after taking that first Zumba class, Yulissa made her dream come true by becoming the first person with Down syndrome to be certified to teach Zumba in the United States. Now, she teaches several classes every week all over California and has traveled as far as Anchorage, Alaska, to teach classes.

The two biggest moments for Yulissa on her amazing dance journey have been leading a session with the founder of Zumba, Beta Perez, at the Zumba Instructor Convention in Orlando, Florida, and serving as Grand Marshal and Special Guest of the 6th Annual Step Up for Down syndrome Awareness Walk.

Yulissa is some of the best things to be in the world – self-motivated, energetic, and fun.

"Talent...that's all I've got!"

If there is one thing Zack is not short of it is confidence after all he made first acting appearance as the star of a video about how the stork delivers babies to mommies all around the world. Before long, he progressed to playing a frog in a play at age three. When he was a ready for school, the school district told his mommy that they did not accept children like him. Zack's mommy did not think this was fair, so she went to a place called Office of Civil Rights to ask for help. They fought hard and won; Zack became the first child with Down Syndrome to be fully included in the Palm Beach County school district. With his mommy by his side as his loudest cheerleader, Zack graduated from high school and college as a theater major.

Never afraid to speak for himself or for others, it was not a surprise that while filming with the nonprofit film production company Zeno Mountain Farm, he asked two guest film makers to make a film with him as the star. The filmmakers were so impressed with his talent and charisma that they wrote a script called The Peanut Butter Falcon incorporating many of Zack's expressions, mannerisms but especially his joy, warmth, optimism, and enthusiasm. This film became Zack's first feature film for which he received many awards such as the Hollywood Critics Association Newcomer Award, Breaththrough Entertainer Award from the Associated Press, the Quincy Jones Exceptional Advocate Award from the Global Down Syndrome Foundation, etc. In 2020, he became the first person with Down Syndrome to be a presenter at the Academy Awards after which he was invited to Norway to speak on World Down Syndrome Day.

Zack has many hobbies that include playing basketball, swimming, kayaking, bowling, windsurfing etc. He lives independently and is a leader in the group Self Advocate for Independent Living (SAIL). While he continues to expand his reach in the performing arts, Zack continues to advocate for the rights of people with disabilities in many ways including by exercising his right to vote in every election.

Zack is some of the best things to be in the world – enthusiastic, independent, and bold. Self Advocate for Independent Living (SAIL). While he continues to expand his reach in the performing arts, Zack also advocates for the rights of people with disabilities in many ways including exercising his right to vote in every election.

Zack is some of the best things to be in the world – enthusiastic, independent, and bold.

Chelsea Werner

"I'm a very positive person and don't see things as limitations."

When Chelsea's parents were expecting her, they did not expect any surprises after all she would be their third child. When she finally arrived, her parents realized that their journey was going to be more scenic, and they looked forward to the new things they would learn with her as their guide. Chelsea did not walk until she was almost two years old. Her mommy and daddy told her every day that she could walk and when she began to take small steps, they cheered for her. Soon she was having so much fun walking, then running, and after a while no one could catch her!

Born in Danville, California, Chelsea liked to have fun playing soccer, baseball, swimming. She found her love, though, when she tried gymnastics and a door magically opened into another world where she could fly! It was not easy because it would take her years to learn skills that would normally take a gymnast a year to learn, for example, it took her five years to learn and perform a move called the kip. She never gave up, and for her the fun really started when she discovered the floor routines that allowed her to show the world why her dad gave her the nickname "Showtime."

Chelsea was eight when she began training, and by age thirteen, she was entering competitions. At first, she would come in last place at the competitions but with focus, determination, and hard work she flipped those scores and started to win games and hearts across the country.

Now, at age twenty-eight, Chelsea is not only a four-time National Champion of the Special Olympics and a three-time World Champion, but is also a model for H&M, Adidas, Tommy Hilfiger, Target, Teen Vogue, and more.

Chelsea is some of the best things to be in the world – tenacious, patient, and brave.

DeOndra Dixon

> **"I know my family loves me. They never set limits and always make me feel like I can touch the sky."**

DeOndra has a famous sibling, but she has always been the star of her family. Her brother would take her everywhere with him and even though he was a celebrity, people were more interested in meeting DeOndra. When she was born in Dallas, Texas, her daddy told her that he was scared and confused because he did not know anything about Down syndrome. One day, he was reading a poem, and the line, "God gave special children to special parents," lit up like a beaming jedi sword. It reminded him that DeOndra was his special princess, and he was the knight that would protect her.

While her daddy was a little scared, her mother was the very opposite. She told DeOndra that there was nothing different about her. Her mommy told her to go out in the world and have fun doing what other kids were doing. Without hesitation DeOndra took on the challenge like a champion. She was fearless on the school bus, on the playground and the classroom where she showed that she could keep up with the other kids and graduated with her high school class. Next, she participated in the Special Olympics winning multiple awards and medals.

Like every other girl her age, DeOndra had dreams that she wished would come true—to be a professional dancer, marry Chris Brown, and meet President Barack Obama. Although she never received professional training as a dancer, her natural ability and star quality paved the way for her to dance in music videos, concerts, and even at the Grammy Awards in front of twenty-five million people. Besides dancing, DeOndra's other passion in life was advocacy, both for herself and for others with Down syndrome. She was enormously proud to be appointed a Global Down Syndrome Foundation Ambassador, to serve as the inspiration for and be the first recipient of the Quincy Jones Exceptional Advocacy Award.

DeOndra is some of the best things to be in the world – magnetic, irrepressible and a beacon of hope.

"We need to see more people with a learning disability in the media. It's so important. We deserve equal opportunities like you all do, jobs like you all have. We need to be celebrated because we're people, we exist."

Originally from the city of Leeds in England, George attended mainstream schools from primary school through high school. He received his General Certificate of Secondary Education (high school diploma) in Media, Math, English, Food Tech, and a sports qualification before studying Creative Digital Media Production in college.

When George was eight years old, he started acting at StageDoor Theater and Music school and took part in many shows, but his first acting role in a film was S.A.M., a film about two boys called Sam from different backgrounds who bond on the swings at a park. He also made an appearance in the sci-fi short film "BEBE A.I."

As an actor and dancer, George is passionate about representation on stage and screen. He is part of a national theater ensemble with Separate Doors, works with Yorkshire Dance, and is part of the performance academy at Mind the Gap Studios, studying for a performing arts degree.

George is an ambassador for Parkrun and Mencap. While working for Mencap, he worked on some projects with their TV program which led to shooting a video for BBC Bitesize on the "five myths of Down's syndrome," which went viral. Because the video was successful, BBC asked George to audition for CBeebies, the British equivalent of Sesame Street. One month later, George received the amazing news that he would be the first BBC children's presenter with Down syndrome. And with that, George Webster's dream exploded into reality.

The best part of the announcement was that his disability was not mentioned, he was introduced to the world simply as George, a young man who loves to cook, sing, and dance. He wants to further his acting career and would love to appear in the popular show Doctor Who or a James Bond film. A huge fan of the dance show Come Strictly Dancing, he said he would jump at the chance to show his dance moves on the series.

George is some of the best things in the world to be – engaging, sharp, and interesting.

George
Webster

Angela Bachiller

"I've always voted since I was eighteen years old, but other people (in my situation) have never been able to. We want the laws relating to the right to vote changed. I want to be an honest politician"

Angela was born in Valladolid, Spain to parents who did not over protect her, but she also never lacked support since they always encouraged her to live a life of adventure and courage. She played with friends at the park, enjoyed sports, and as she grew older, she went to movies, restaurants, and traveled all over Europe independently. Her parents also believed strongly in education; they made sure she started school at the early age of one.

Angela had worked as an administrative assistant for three years at the Valladolid City Hall and took up the chance to serve when a member of the People's Party decided to step down from the position. This action took a lot of courage since some people do not think people with Down syndrome can hold important jobs like working in a political office. Angela did not pay attention to what anyone had to say, she knew this was a chance to advocate for people like herself in government.

On July 29, 2013, she was sworn in as city councilor for Valladolid and a member of the People's Party making her the first person with Down syndrome to hold a political office. Angela's appointment was fully supported by everyone in her town. They thought that her participation in governance would encourage other people like her to play a bigger part in society so they can also control their destiny.

Angela is determined to use her authority to ensure that enough money is in place to help fund quality education for people with disabilities throughout Spain. She wants everyone to know that people with Down syndrome should not be limited to other people's definition of success.

When she is not maneuvering the halls of power, Angela loves her Latin dancing, English, and music theory classes. She also plays the piano and loves to read. She has read El Quijote (Don Quixote) three times!

Angela is some of the best things to be in the world – remarkable, friendly, and empowered.

"If people make fun of me or my friends it's more their loss and their problem than mine."

When James Martin was born, the doctors told his mommy and daddy that he would probably never speak. But once he got started, he never stopped, and it has been the sweetest sound to their ears.

James, who is a Mencap ambassador, was a student at Harberton Special School in Belfast, Ireland. When he was fourteen he joined the Babosh theater company, an acting group for children with learning disabilities. James became sure of two things—he had found a home, and he really wanted to be an actor like Robert De Niro and his Irish heroes Liam Neeson, James Nesbitt, and Jamie Dornan.

James was never given a limit on how far his dream could go. All his mommy and daddy wanted for him was happiness and a sense of satisfaction in the life he chooses to create for himself. His first leading role was in the BBC drama Ups and Downs for which he won a best actor gong at the New York City TV festival. Next, he appeared in the Netflix series Marcella before landing the role of Lorcan in the short film, An Irish Goodbye, which won the award for best live action movie at the 2023 BAFTA in London and the Academy Awards. This made James the first person with Down syndrome to win an Oscar. This award was also very special because it was given to him on his thirty-first birthday and all the famous celebrities in the audience sang "Happy Birthday" to him!

James, who loves to run and play the harmonica, has worked as a barista at Starbucks and a chef at a restaurant for the last ten years and has no plans of stopping until the next role comes calling.

James is some of the best things to be in the world – brilliant, stylish, and charming.

James Martin

"No matter who you are, you can make a difference in this world."

Born in Ridgefield, Connecticut, Colette started baking when she was four years old with her mommy who always encouraged her to learn new things. As she grew older, she was sad as her brother and sister made new friends while she was bullied in school. Nobody invited her for sleepovers or birthday tea parties. Colette continued to bake. It made her feel good, like she had something special of her own, too.

After high school, she graduated from the LIFE program at Clemson University. LIFE stands for Learning Is for Everyone, which is not always true for people with Down syndrome like Colette. She was ready to be independent, but it was hard to find a job since she was always told that she was not a good fit. Colette made a very important decision. She did not have to fit in, she did not have to wait for anyone to choose her, she would turn her love of baking into a business.

With the help of her mommy and sister, Colette DeVito started her company, Collettey's Cookies. She delivered samples of cookies in various flavors to a local store. To her delight, her recipe for the chocolate chip and cinnamon cookies called "The Amazing Cookie" was a success! At first, she was worried about completing her first large order, but worry was soon won over by experience and confidence.

Before long, everyone not only loved her cookies, but they wanted to know about the capable young woman who created the company. She has shared her story on CNN, Good Morning America, Inside Edition, CBS Evening News, ABC World News, People Magazine, and more reaching people all around the world.

Collettey's Cookies has sold over 400,000 cookies online and in seven different stores, and earned $1.2 million dollars! To Colette, the most important achievement of her company is that it has hired fifteen people with diverse needs whom she trains personally.

Colette is some of the best things to be in the world – candid, dedicated, and spirited.

Colette Devito

Pablo Pineda

> **"Down syndrome does not define me nor conditions me, people judge a book by its cover, including me.**
> **Prejudices come from not knowing enough."**

Pablo is on the list of famous citizens of Malaga, Spain, along with famous artist Pablo Picasso and actor Antonio Banderas. At first, only his daddy knew his secret: he was a homie with the extra chromie! It did not change how he felt about his son. When his mommy finally realized that he carried the extra chromosome, she thought it made him extra special, like seeing a unicorn at the end of a rainbow. They showered him with love and attention, as did his three brothers who could not wait to teach him everything they knew about being kids. His dad was a theater director, and he would read books to Pablo and taught him many different languages, including Latin, while his mother would talk to him about life and the world. They never let him use his diagnosis as a reason not to do his best.

Pablo started school at five where he impressed his teachers with the sharpness of his mind and the depth of his thoughts. It was also at school that he learned that he was considered "different." When he was seven, his teacher told him that he had Down syndrome. Pablo asked the teacher if that meant that he was not smart, and the teacher said no. That was all Pablo needed to hear! From then on, he stopped paying attention to Down syndrome or letting people use it to define him.

Pablo is the only person in Europe with Down syndrome that has a college degree, and several diplomas in art and educational psychology. He is also the only professor with Down syndrome, and the only Spanish person with Down syndrome to play the main role in a film (Y Tu Mama Tambien) for which he won multiple awards.

When he is not writing (he has written two books) and teaching, he travels across the world to advocate for employment for people with disabilities. Currently, he is working with the Adecco Foundation to develop a program that will help to include people with disabilities in all areas of society. After all, nobody wants to feel lonely or left out of fun things.

Pablo is some of the best things to be in the world – daring, humorous, and unstoppable.

Anoushka's
Extraordinary Heroes is an
inspirational book about individuals with
Down syndrome who live fulfilling lives with
strength, bravery, resilience and determination in spite
of their challenges. It sheds light on individuals with
Down syndrome who are contributing members of society
in major industries such as the restaurant business, fashion,
entertainment, art, education, politics, etc. This book defies
the persistent underestimation of people with intellectual and
developmental disabilities. Anoushka's Extraordinary Heroes
seeks to encourage individuals with Down syndrome and
their families to reject limitations placed on their lives
by society and to encourage others outside of the
Lucky Few community to value and respect
them.

About the Author

Ebbe Bassey is a civil servant, actor, producer and above all the mom of and advocate for the fiercely independent sassy miss Anoushka [aka Warrior Princess Mini Diva] who has been the inspiration for everything in her world since her near debut on the A train. The author resides in Fairfield, CT with her science educator-musician-hockey goalie but mostly amazing husband, Mark Manczuk. Nope, no pets.